LEMURS
of MADAGASCAR

Find our books at Amazon, Barnes & Nobles, Walmart, Books-A-Million, OverDrive, IngramSpark, Lulu and more!

Like, Share and Follow us on Facebook, Instagram, Twitter, Pinterest, YouTube, LinkedIn, Spotify, Apple Podcast and more!

www.SlothDreamsBooks.com

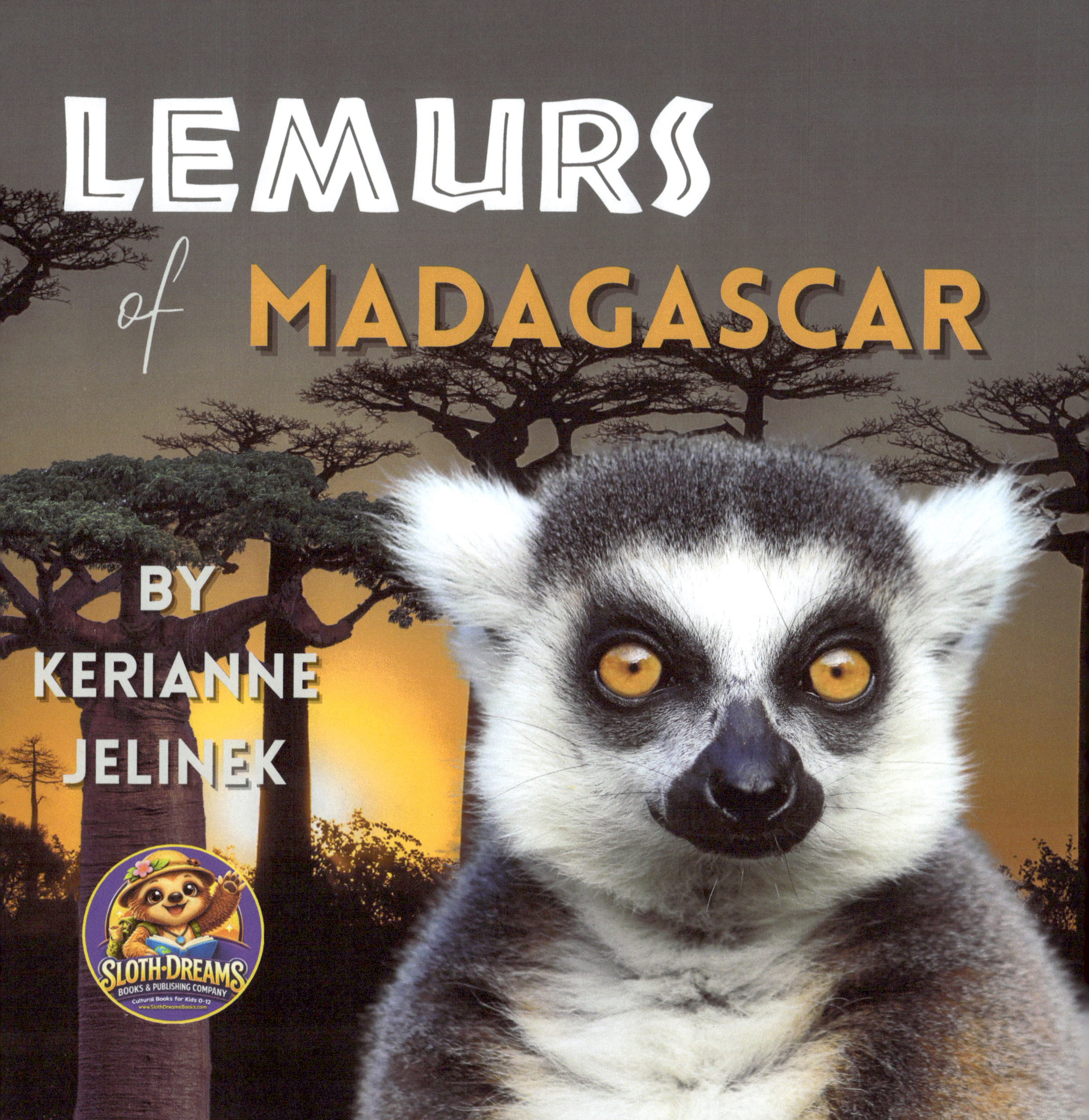

LEMURS
of MADAGASCAR
BY KERIANNE JELINEK
SLOTH·DREAMS
BOOKS & PUBLISHING COMPANY
Cultural Books for Kids 0-12
www.SlothDreamsBooks.com

WHAT ARE LEMURS?

Lemurs are primates found only on the island of Madagascar, off the southeastern coast of Africa. They belong to the Lemuriformes family and are known for their unique appearance and behavior. Lemurs are mammals. They give birth to live babies.

THIS IS A RING-
TAILED LEMUR

Where do Lemurs live?

Lemurs inhabit various ecosystems in Madagascar, including rainforests, dry forests, and even spiny forests. They are adapted to a wide range of habitats, from lush forests to arid regions.

What is Madagascar?

Madagascar is an island country surrounded by water. It has tropical beaches, rainforest, and arid dry forests. It is a beautiful country. Madagascar is off of the coast of South–Eastern Africa.

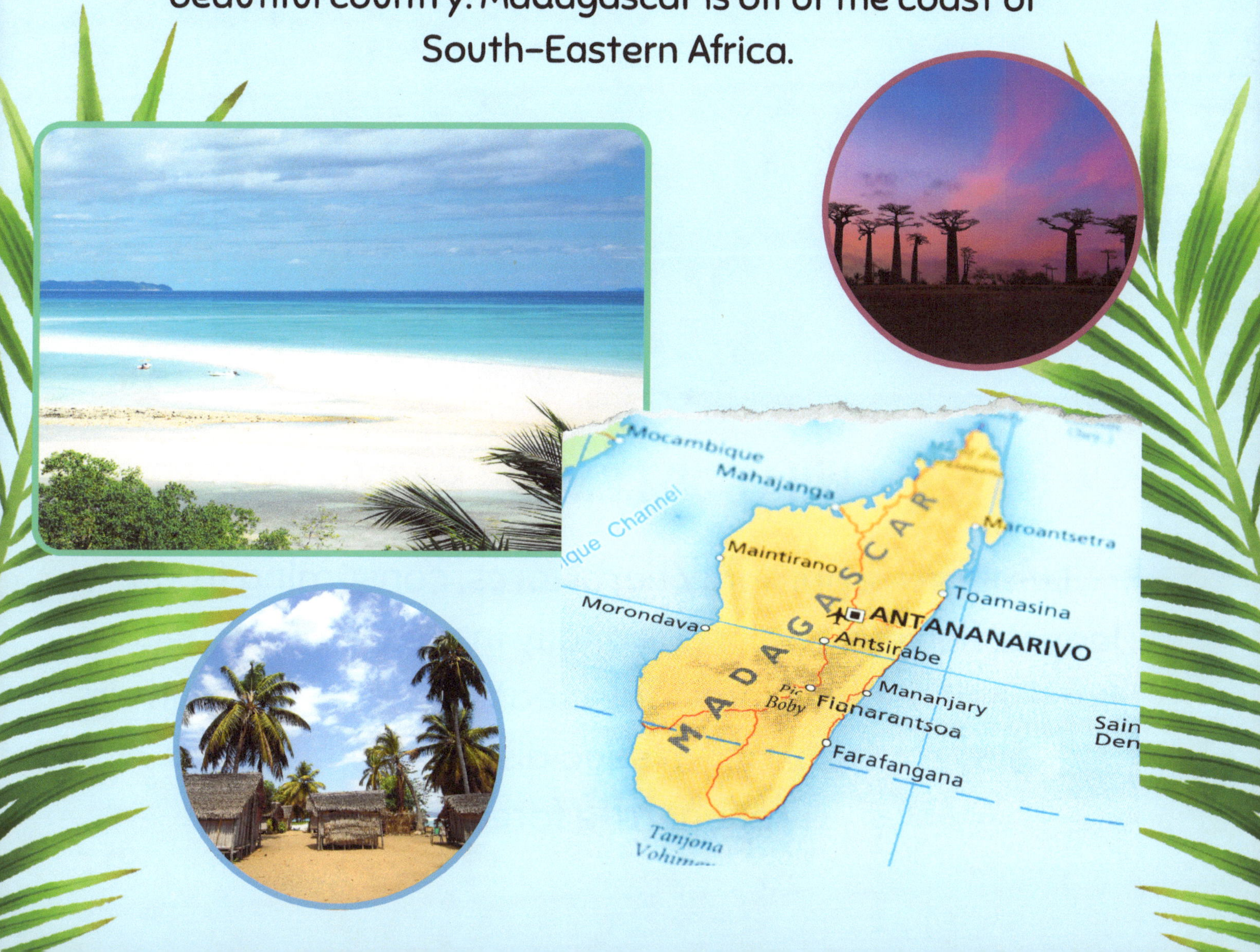

WHAT DO LEMURS EAT?

Lemurs are primarily herbivores, consuming fruits, leaves, flowers, and occasionally insects. Some species, like the ring-tailed lemur, also eat bark and sap. Lemurs play a crucial role in seed dispersal, helping to regenerate forests.

Yummy Fruit,
Sap & Bugs!

What are their behaviors?

Lemurs are known for their social structures, with many species living in groups called troops. They communicate through vocalizations, scent marking, and body language. Some lemurs, like the sifakas, are known for their unique way of leaping through the trees.

LEAPIN' LEMURS!!
OH, HELLO THERE!

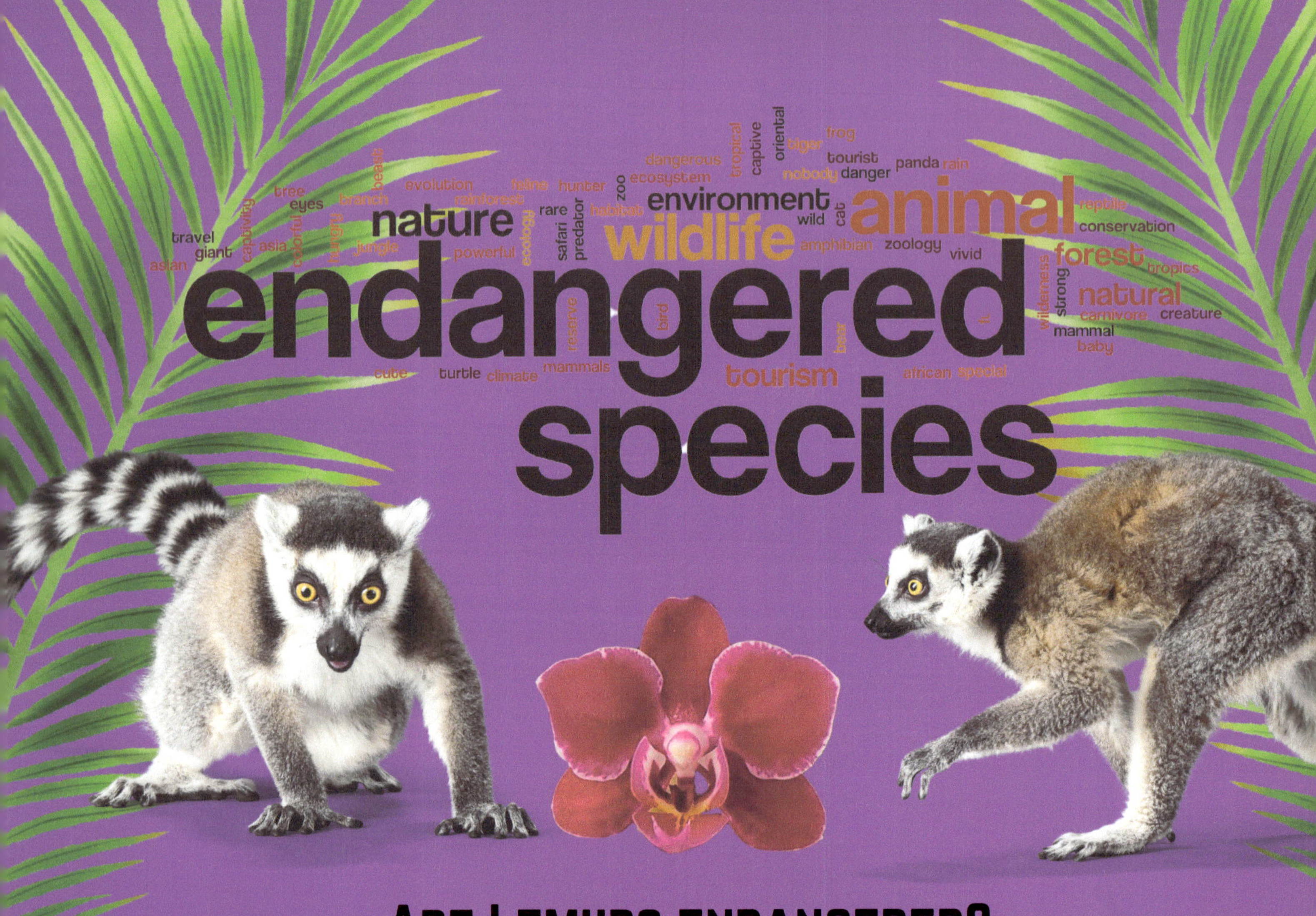

Are Lemurs endangered?

Unfortunately, many lemur species are endangered due to habitat loss, hunting, and illegal pet trade. Conservation efforts are underway to protect their habitats and raise awareness about these animals.

ENDANGERED
SPECIES
!

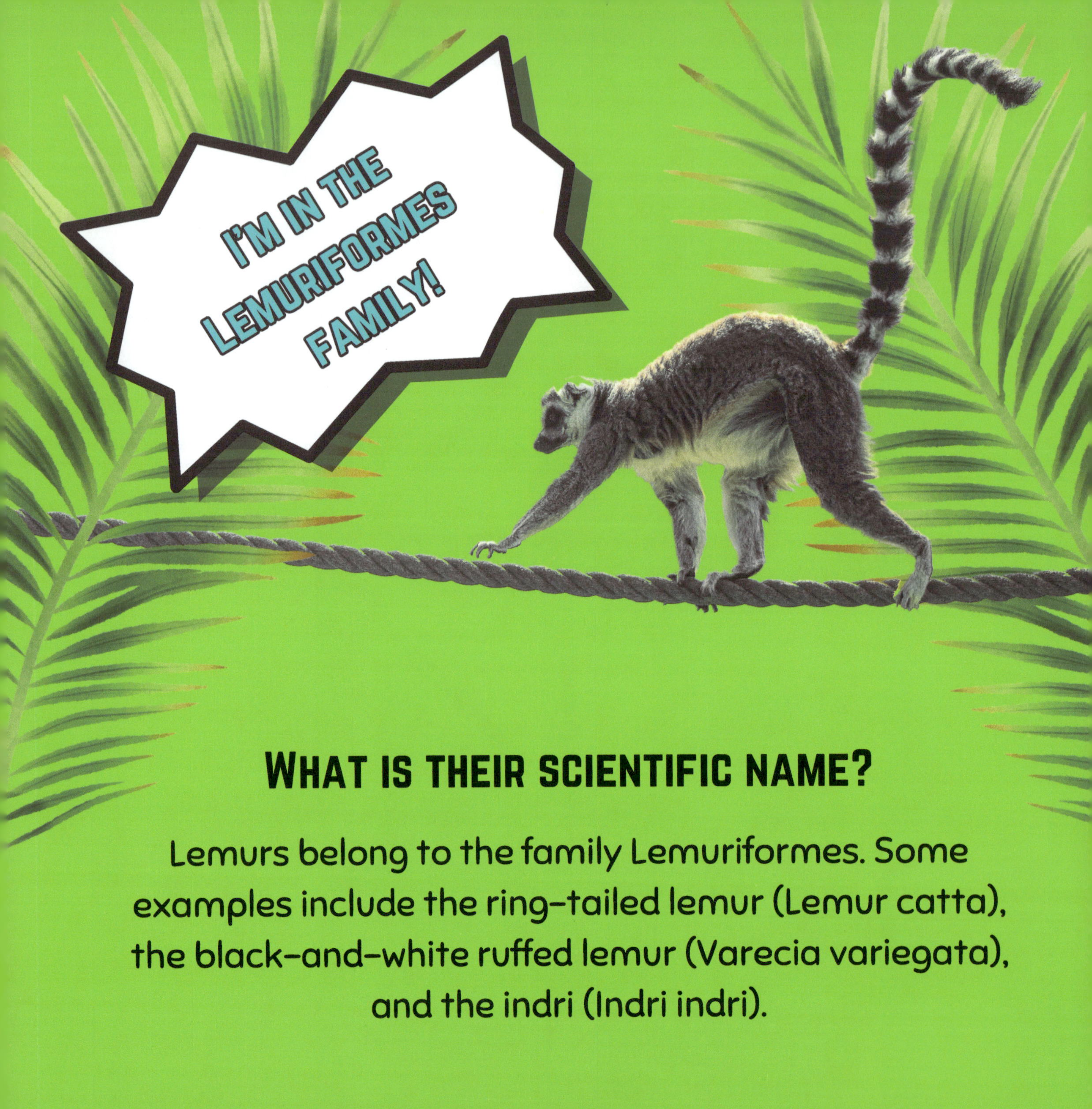

WHAT IS THEIR SCIENTIFIC NAME?

Lemurs belong to the family Lemuriformes. Some examples include the ring-tailed lemur (Lemur catta), the black-and-white ruffed lemur (Varecia variegata), and the indri (Indri indri).

WE ARE SO CUTE!

Ring-Tailed Lemur (Lemur catta):

Meet the Ring-Tailed Lemur, known for its distinctive black and white ringed tail. These lemurs love to eat fruits, leaves, and even insects. Unfortunately, they face habitat loss due to deforestation, making them an endangered species.

Red Ruffed Lemur (Varecia rubra):

With vibrant red fur and a loud call, the Red Ruffed Lemur is a sight to behold. Found in Madagascar's rainforests, they enjoy feasting on fruits, nectar, and flowers. However, their numbers are declining due to habitat destruction and hunting.

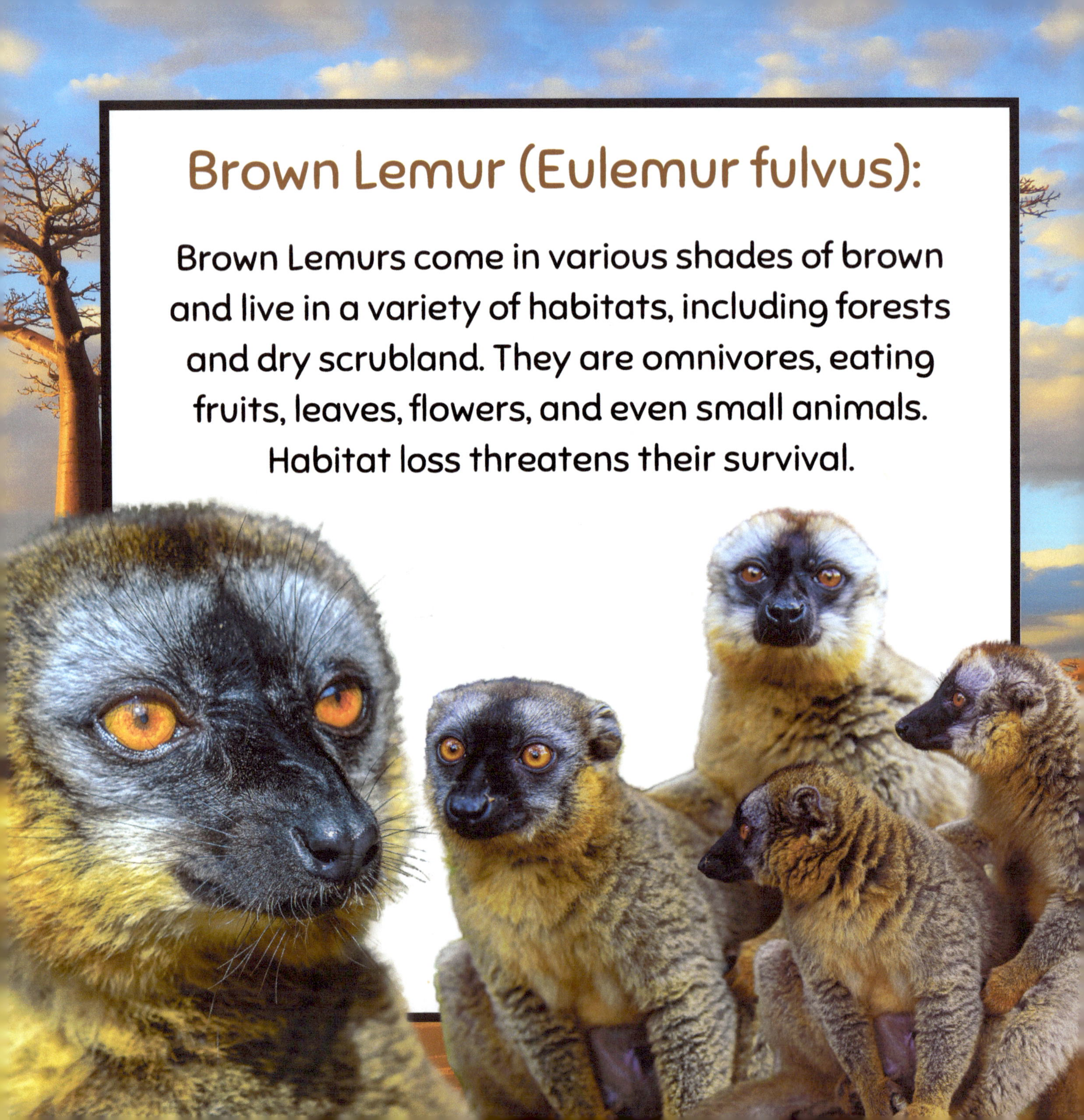

Brown Lemur (Eulemur fulvus):

Brown Lemurs come in various shades of brown and live in a variety of habitats, including forests and dry scrubland. They are omnivores, eating fruits, leaves, flowers, and even small animals. Habitat loss threatens their survival.

Indri (Indri indri):

The Indri is the largest lemur species, known for its unique singing ability. These black and white lemurs primarily eat leaves and live high up in the trees of Madagascar's forests. Sadly, they are critically endangered due to deforestation.

Mouse Lemur (Microcebus):

Despite their tiny size, Mouse Lemurs play a big role in Madagascar's ecosystems. These nocturnal lemurs feed on insects, fruits, and flowers. They face threats from habitat loss and climate change.

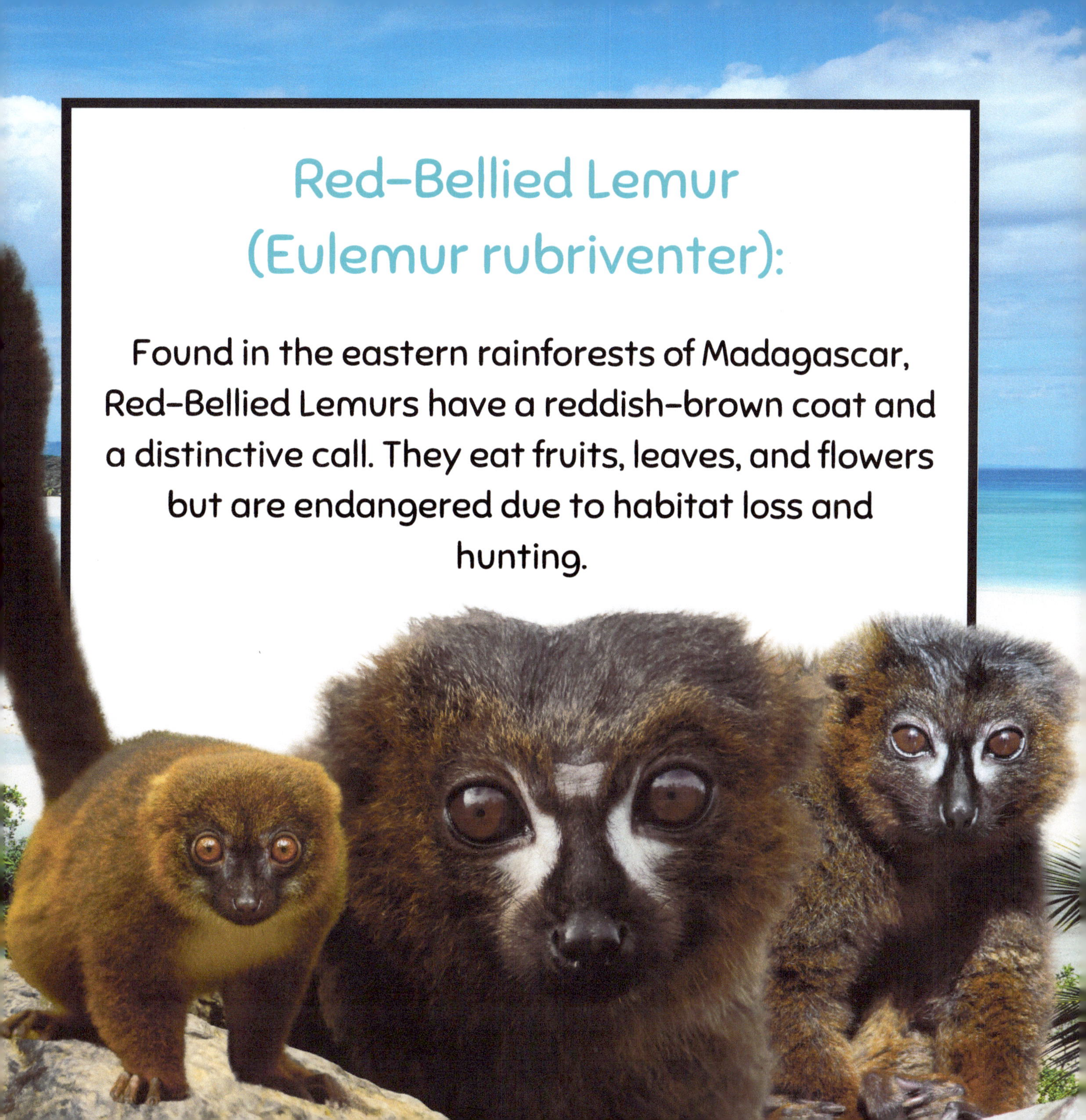

Red-Bellied Lemur (Eulemur rubriventer):

Found in the eastern rainforests of Madagascar, Red-Bellied Lemurs have a reddish-brown coat and a distinctive call. They eat fruits, leaves, and flowers but are endangered due to habitat loss and hunting.

Golden Bamboo Lemur (Hapalemur aureus):

As their name suggests, Golden Bamboo Lemurs have a golden-orange fur coat. They primarily eat bamboo, which is quite rare among lemurs. Habitat destruction threatens their bamboo habitats, endangering their survival.

Sifaka (Propithecus):

Sifakas are known for their unique way of moving by hopping sideways on the ground. They mainly eat leaves and live in the forests of Madagascar. Habitat destruction threatens their survival.

Diademed Sifaka (Propithecus diadema):

Diademed Sifakas are known for their beautiful golden crowns and white fur. They inhabit Madagascar's eastern rainforests and primarily eat leaves. Sadly, they are critically endangered due to habitat destruction.

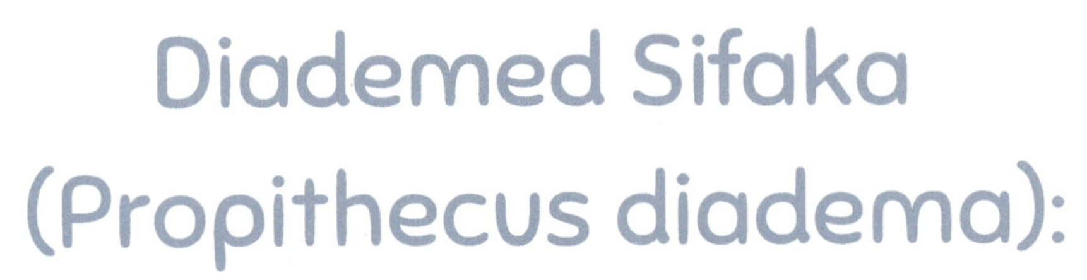

Black-and-White Ruffed Lemur (Varecia variegata):

Sporting a striking coat of black and white fur, these lemurs are famous for their loud vocalizations. They dine on fruits, leaves, and nectar. Unfortunately, they are endangered due to habitat loss and hunting.

Coquerel's Sifaka (Propithecus coquereli):

Named after the French naturalist Charles Coquerel, these lemurs have a golden-brown coat with white patches on their shoulders. They primarily feed on leaves and face threats from habitat destruction.

Giant Mouse Lemur (Mirza):

Despite their name, Giant Mouse Lemurs are still quite small compared to other lemurs. They are nocturnal and feed on insects, fruits, and flowers. Their populations are declining due to habitat loss.

Aye-Aye
(Daubentonia madagascariensis):

With its large eyes and long, bony finger, the Aye-Aye is one of Madagascar's most unusual lemurs. It uses its finger to tap on trees and find grubs to eat. Sadly, they are endangered due to superstitions and habitat loss.

Greater Bamboo Lemur
(Prolemur simus):

Greater Bamboo Lemurs are specialized bamboo eaters, with adaptations to digest bamboo's tough fibers. Unfortunately, they are critically endangered due to habitat loss and hunting.

Crowned Lemur
(Eulemur coronatus):

These lemurs have a distinctive orange crown on their head, making them easily recognizable. They enjoy dining on fruits, leaves, and flowers. However, habitat loss poses a significant threat to their survival.

LEMURS
of
MADAGASCAR

I LOVE LEMURS!

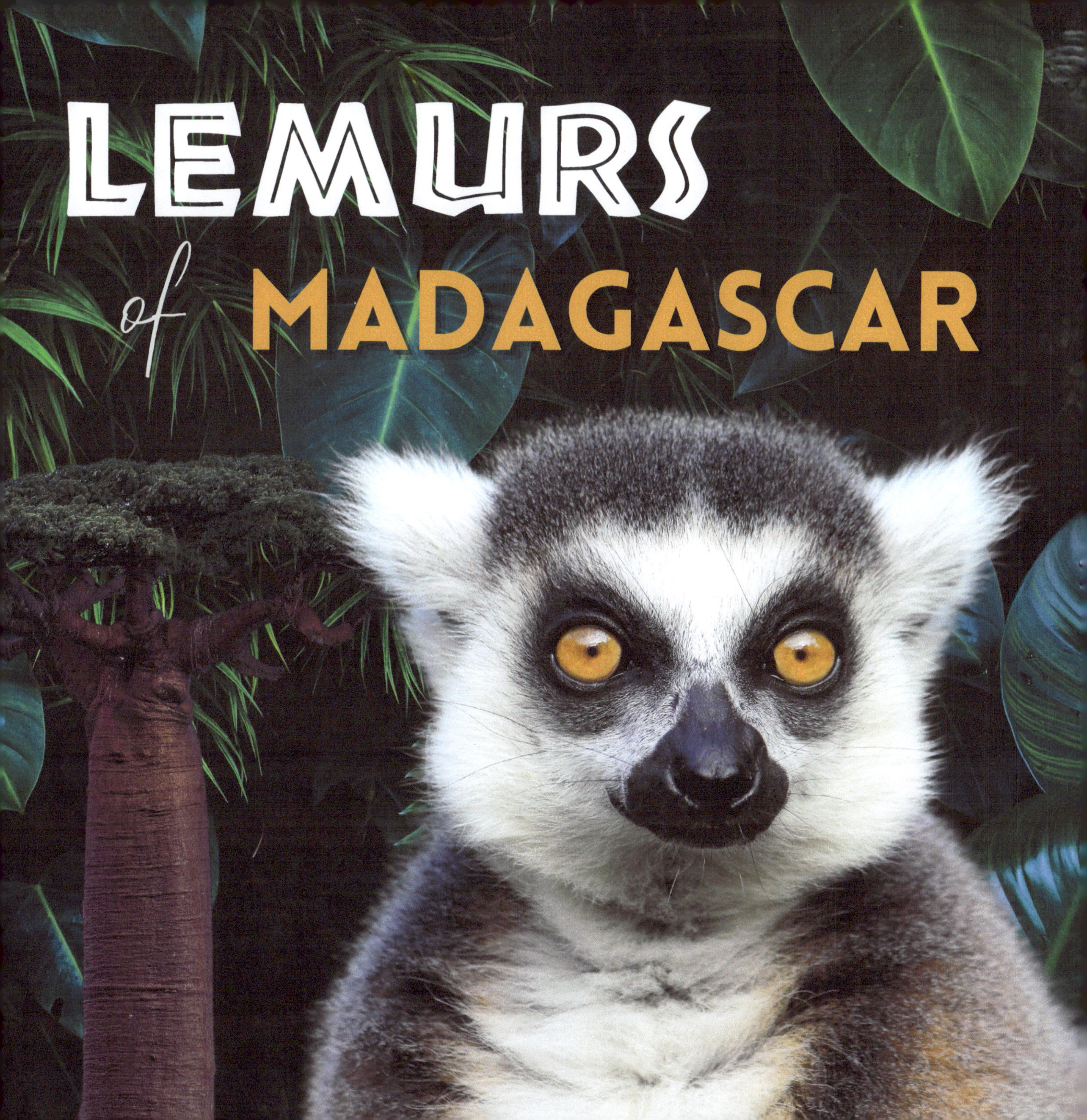

LEMURS
of
MADAGASCAR

9 784618 539831